ASHINGTON

A History in Photographs

Selected and annotated by Bill Harrison

Northumberland Library

First published in 1990 by Northumberland County Library,
The Willows, Morpeth, Northumberland
NE61 1TA.

Copyright © B Harrison and Northumberland County Library
1990

All rights reserved

Printed by Unit Offset Group, Newcastle upon Tyne

British Library Cataloguing in Publication Data

Harrison, Bill 1928 –

Ashington: A History in Photographs
1. English photographs. Special subjects: London
I. Title. II. Northumberland County Library
779.9942886

ISBN 0 9513027 7 9

INTRODUCTION

Ashington is situated some two and a half miles inland from the North Sea, and is bounded on the south by the River Wansbeck and on the north-east and west by agricultural land. In the middle of the last century it was described as being pleasantly situated in the midst of an open stretch of country, and as a colliery village was known as Felham Down. Within a few years the seat of mining operations had moved half a mile to the east and the original shaft had ceased to be used as a coal-raising shaft. A newspaper article in 1873 said 'where formerly only a few small landsale pits existed we now see large collieries with gigantic pit gearing and towering chimneys that belch forth clouds of thick black smoke, and where formerly, a few wretched hovels marked the site of a colliery village, we now see comfortable brick cottages springing up like blue-topped mushrooms. On a spot where a few short years ago there were nothing but green fields, and the work of the farmer there will soon be a large village'.

The land on which the colliery was sunk belonged to the Duke of Portland, and restrictions were placed on the building of schools and shops. The residents were also barred from using paths through the fields, and a reporter said: 'It is to be hoped that Ashingtonians will stick to their right of way: for however important it may be that hares shall breed unmolested to provide sport for the leisure hours of the aristocratic person it is of much greater importance that the small rights of way which the public still possess should be protected'.

With the rapid development of the collieries the old ways had to change, and what was regarded as a model town was built. With the exception of the Second Row each of the rows of colliery houses faced south, and at the back of the houses was a road 20 feet wide across which stood the toilets and coalhouses. A seven foot high wall separated the outhouses from the 30 yards long garden of the next row of houses. Ten miles of tramway by which household coal was brought to each house, and refuse removed, covered the area.

Until 1896 Ashington was supervised and controlled by Morpeth Rural Council, but had its own Parish Council. It was then realised that this was not an effective way to administer the fast growing town, and on 4 December 1896 a special meeting was called by the Parish Council with a view to rearranging and enlarging the parish of Ashington. In 1896 Ashington was constituted an Urban District, and in 1914 the parishes of Ashington and Hirst amalgamated forming one parish of Ashington.

The new council faced a daunting task for the town had been built to serve the needs of the colliery. The lack of suitable offices and buildings was eventually overcome and it was decided that the seal of the local authority would be a representation of the Duke Pit Heapstead. There were arguments about whether the inscription *'Labour Conquers All'* should be in Latin or English, but eventually the scholars won and the seal with its Latin inscription is still used today.

Although the Coal Company was imaginative and progressive in many ways, the owners ignored the poor living conditions of their workers. The town's Medical Officers regularly complained about the poor water supply, lack of pavements and made up roads, and stressed the need for public baths and water closets. With the larger population sewage disposal became a serious problem, for the sewage of the district was being put into the Haydon Letch and River Wansbeck untreated. In 1922 the Council instructed civil engineers to prepare a scheme of main drainage for the whole of the Urban District, and the work was completed in 1927. Public lighting was improved, the electric street lighting being supplied by the Northern Counties Electricity Supply Limited. The Tynemouth Corporation supplied drinking water whilst slop or sludge water was taken from the Ashington Coal Company for the purpose of street watering, and flushing of sewers. Main roads were surfaced with asphalt or tarmacadam, but until the 1930's a large number of private streets were in poor repair for the privy middens were being converted into water closets, and the work was delayed because of the necessity of laying water branches and drains.

By the 1940's the living conditions of the residents had greatly improved as electric washers, vacuum cleaners and electrical irons replaced the poss-tubs, mangles and brooms. There were pithead baths at each of the Company's collieries except Ashington itself, for the workers had decided they would rather have swimming baths. It was not until after the end of the Second World War that the Ashington miners were able to have a bath at the pit, and the days of a bath in a zinc tub in front of a roaring fire were gone forever.

I would like to thank British Coal for allowing me to publish photographs from the records of the Ashington Coal Company.

The mushroom growth of housing, and increased population created opportunities for businessmen, and shops were built at what was to be called High Market or Market Place. Before that time people bought their everyday needs from hawkers or residents who ran small businesses in their own homes. The Fairley family sold newspapers in the Third Row, Ellen Dickinson was a butcher at Glebe Cottage, Thomas Marshall a chemist in Ninth Row and Hugh Singer mended shoes in the Fifth Row. After the shops were built people travelled from Pegswood, Guidepost and other villages in the area to do their shopping. The local authority offices were in Market Place, and their surveyor Alexander Wood had a reputation for being a brilliant cartoonist. He enjoyed drawing cartoons of candidates at the local elections, and whilst they amused the electorate some of them annoyed the prospective councillors.

The first houses in Long Row were built in 1852, and by 1857 the Row had been completed. It consisted of 33 'back-to-back' houses, each having four rooms but a dividing wall separated the front two rooms from the back two rooms with the result that two families occupied each of the houses. In 1859 a pantry was added to the back and the front of each house. The dividing wall between the houses was very thin, and there wasn't much privacy for the occupiers. In 1884 the houses were altered and the dividing wall removed, allowing one family to occupy the four-room houses, the other family being rehoused elsewhere. The company spent £2,126 on these alterations, and similar changes to houses in Cross Row.

Florrie Anderson hanging the washing out in her garden in Long Row. She was lucky she had this space for the back lanes were usually inches deep in mud or dust. Her house had a rain barrel in the back yard, and the rain water was used to wash the clothes and also her hair for the water was nice and soft. Each of the houses had two bedrooms and two rooms downstairs. Their food was stored in a small pantry. When the family first moved in there wasn't a staircase, and the Andersons had to climb a ladder to reach their bedrooms. The dormer window was a later addition to the house replacing a very small bedroom window. Many of the miners in the row grew leeks in their gardens, and there was a great deal of rivalry between them as they attempted to win first prize at one of the clubs.

Mary Ann Gardner, daughter Kate and a neighbour having a good laugh in the back lane at Long Row. Large families were commonplace 80 years ago and Will and Mary Gardner had seven children. Kate started work when she was 14 years of age at the Co-operative Store. She was employed in the tailoring department making shirts, and the first thing she had to make was a 'laying out' shirt. There wasn't much money to spare, but relatives always tried to give the deceased a good send off! She later worked as a bus conductress for United, and in her spare time played the piano. A member of the Harmonic Band she also played for a small band at dances, and was paid 2/6d an hour for a late night dance and given her supper.

The Parish Church and Co-operative Store at the end of Station Road. The New Pit Co-operative Society was established in 1876 at the end of the Third Row, and the Old Pit Co-operative Society had a shop at the end of Cross Row. They later amalgamated to form the Ashington Industrial Co-operative Society in this new building near the parish church. The Co-operative movement had a strong hold in the town, and although by 1928 there were around 200 privately owned shops the Society dealt with 50% of the shopping trade in the district. In 1928 the Vicar at Ashington Parish Church asked the Coal Company *'for financial assistance towards the erection of a peal of bells with a tower and clock'*, but was told that in the present circumstances such outlay was quite unnecessary.

The Miners Hall, one of the few notable buildings in the town. When the theatre was built the workmen buried a *'message to prosperity'* which had been written by members of the Ashington Miners Committee. The message, old newspapers, a poster describing the foundation laying ceremony and a memorandum from the Ashington Lodge of the Northumberland Miners' Association were discovered when the Hall was rebuilt as the Regal Cinema in 1939. The newspapers described some of the events which were held to commemorate the occasion. A *'Grand Ball'* was held in the Recreation Hall followed by tea in the Portland Hall. Admission to the dance, music being provided by the Orchestral Band, was one shilling per couple.

There were very few buildings to be seen in Hirst in 1906. The land east of the railway station was a purely agricultural area until 1890, but as the land around the colliery became filled up the mining community had to be housed on the nearest available land which was at Hirst. Colliery houses continued to be built until 1910, but the Company ignored the bad state of the roads and poor street lighting. In 1895 the Chairman of Ashington Parish Council *'requested that the Colliery village of Ashington, and the main road from Bothal School to the railway station be lit by gas lamps'*. The Company agreed and erected 32 gas lamps to help solve the problem.

Although the sight of children walking around in bare feet at a seaside resort like Newbiggin would be regarded as quite normal it seems out of place in Station Road, Ashington. The shoeless boy, and the other well dressed children reflect the gulf between rich and poor in 1911. Although miners and their families lived in rent free houses and received concessionary coal for heating and cooking, their wages were poor and after they had bought their food there wasn't much left for clothing. They relied mainly on cheap food like bread, and for those families the price of food was very important indeed. People bought frozen meat from Argentina for it was half the price of British meat, and much of the other food they ate was imported because it was cheaper than food produced in Britain.

Ashington became an Urban District in 1896. A minute in the Coal Company's records reflects the determination of the Company to maintain their influence on the proposed development of the town. It said: *'in view of the nominations of candidates for the newly constituted bodies, it was resolved to secure the nomination and if possible the election of candidates, who are likely to act in harmony with the Company's interests'*. The first council of 15 members included the colliery manager, four colliery officials, four miners and six businessmen and shopkeepers who would follow the Company's policies. The original offices were at the High Market and in 1912 Mr James Strong, Chairman of the Council invited fellow councillors and friends to a dinner at the Portland Hotel to celebrate the opening of these new Council Chambers.

The shopping area west of the Station Bridge. There were regular complaints about the price of goods sold in the shops and one customer asked: *'why London stores were able to send goods to local residents at prices which, including carriage, were lower than those here and how certain firms while helping to make millionaires were able to sell articles at a lower rate than the Co-op'*. The quality of the food which was sold over the counter was also questioned with a fish shop owner being asked: *'if the fish "fresh from Newbiggin" were getting rather a long railway journey before reaching Ashington'*. The regular sales also came in for some criticism when the many bargains in the shops were said to be in reality shoddy goods.

One of the first buildings in Hirst. The large shop standing on its own beside the steep drop to the railway station was owned by J Pedelty and Company, and was known as Portland House. The owners had a printers, newsagents and stationers business, and the shop windows show a wide variety of goods for sale with cards advertising suitable presents for Christmas. There were no other buildings anywhere near on that side of the street, and none at all on the north side. The business in Station Road was later taken over by the Portland House Printing Works Company Limited. The first British picture postcards were published in 1894 and the shop always had a large number in stock. The Edwardians used postcards in the same way that we make telephone calls today and every house had its postcard album for millions were posted each year.

Policemen on duty at the Station Bank. When the colliery was sunk, law and order was maintained by a constable stationed at Morpeth. Robert White who had joined the force of Northumberland Constabulary at its formation in 1857, his number was 10, was then appointed resident policeman. With the rising population and increasing crime, more help was needed, and John Marshall who had joined the force in 1876 was appointed to the town. By 1897 the police station had been built, and it was manned by a sergeant and three constables. In 1902 Sergeant Howey was promoted to Inspector and he was succeeded by Inspector Irving in 1912, Culley in 1914 and Scott in 1927. In those years the population had risen from 2,500 to 29,000 people and the force had increased from a solitary policeman to an inspector, four sergeants and 18 police constables.

In March 1871 contractors were invited to tender for the construction of the line between North Seaton and Newbiggin. Detailed specifications were given in a 35 foolscap page document accompanied by forms on which costings and schedules of quantities had to be shown. The new station was called Hirst, but just as the old colliery name of Felham Down has disappeared from the records so the name Hirst was to suffer a similar fate and quietly disappear from the records of the postal authorities and the railway company, and be replaced by Ashington. The station was very busy at the turn of the century and there were complaints about the service. A letter to a local magazine asked: *'whether staff could be posted at extra exits at the station on Wednesday and Saturday afternoons, and also each evening, and if some of the porters who watch the trains go out would not be better employed at collecting tickets at such extra exits'*.

The town looked prosperous in the early 1920's but the shops weren't taking much money. In March 1921 one million miners were locked out and for the next 13 weeks the men in Ashington were without wages and unemployment benefit. The Morpeth Herald reported that in the town 400 adults and over 1,000 children were suffering extreme hardship and that soup kitchens had been set up to feed them. The Ashington Mineworkers Federation invited all churches, clubs and societies to attend a meeting at the Woodhorn and Linton Miners Hall in order to co-ordinate all activities in the relief of distress amongst women and children. Representatives from the Coal Company attended the meeting where a decision was taken to open depots in different parts of the town.

The Grand Hotel was described as a *'large and beautiful building with a genial host. It has accommodation for every kind of traveller and is a meeting place for many organisations including the Freemasons. It is the convivial centre of the district and entirely worthy of its name – The Grand.'* Many people were annoyed by the poor state of the roads and one resident sarcastically asked *'whether the Ashington Urban District Council would erect notice boards similar to the one at North Seaton Station on all roads leading to Ashington'*. It said *'This road is not suitable for motor traffic, char-a-bancs, horse vehicles, motor cycles, cars, pedestrians etc.'* I suspect he had added the pedestrians bit himself to emphasise his displeasure.

The cellars under the Clock Bar at the Grand Hotel around 1930. The hotel was situated in the centre of the main shopping area and even at that time questions were still being asked about the wisdom of allowing hotels and clubs to operate in the town. There was little money and one paper asked: 'why is it possible in these hard times to meet five drunken men during a walk through one of the streets of Hirst, and if the drunken individual who stood at the Grand Corner sneering at the motor cars has ever realised that he has probably swallowed in alcohol more than sufficient in value to have purchased for himself two cars'.

A beautiful interior with a wonderful dancing floor was how dancers described the Princess Ballroom. It had an oak parquetry floor hung upon spiral springs, a first class band and an expert teacher of dancing who held classes for those wishing to learn to dance. Novelty feature nights, carnivals and fancy dress balls were held regularly, and children were well catered for with ballroom and display dancing classes being held every Saturday afternoon. The cafe in the ballroom could accommodate 250 people at one sitting, and wedding receptions, social functions, football parties and supper dances were catered for. Trade exhibitions, bazaars, concerts and civic functions were held in the large hall. The ballroom was destroyed by fire in April 1944.

Chester Armstrong wrote in his biography 'Pilgrimage to Nenthead' that 'Ashington in 1881 was a colliery village extending no further than the manager's house at the end of the First Row. Limited on the west by the oldest parts of the colliery, the view eastwards from the manager's house was bare of human habitation as far as Woodhorn Village, save for the railway station, just built, Nixon's farm and Low Hirst a farmhouse with cottages adjoining'. Nixon's Farm stood on the edge of the road leading to Woodhorn and the Wallaw Cinema was built on the site of its old open cart sheds. On the opposite side of the road were open fields and two or three farm cottages. In 1936 when it was in the possession of Mr Dungait the farmhouse was demolished in order to make way for the new bus station.

Mr W Gray taking part in the '*turf-cutting*' ceremony which took place on 27 January 1923 as members of the Methodist Church started the work on their new hall. Foundation stones were also laid by Mr T Errel, the Reverend J E Reilly and Harry French who was deputising for his grandfather Pastor W H Thwaites who was too ill to attend. The money needed for its construction was raised in many ways and the fund got off to a good start when a £10,000 donation was given to the Minister. The Coal Company gave £500 and expressed satisfaction that the church was not raising the money needed by means of whist drives and dances.

The Central Hall was opened in May 1924 by Mr Ridley Warham. The Chairman at the public meeting was Mr Joseph Rank who was noted for his generosity in providing money for the construction of Methodist Central Halls. There were several services and meetings to mark the opening of this fine building which was a great improvement on their previous meeting places. The hall was packed for the opening ceremony and tea was provided by the organisers. Sunday School outings were highlights of the year and in 1925 hay carts, rollies and traps which were loaned by the Ashington Co-operative Society took parents and children to Longhirst. The Central Hall Band accompanied them and played all the way to their destination.

Hirst Castle, a fortified farmhouse stood on the side of the road to Woodhorn. What is now Woodhorn Road was then *'a charming country lane through fields of barley and turnips, a romantic route for the young people of that day travelling to and from the dances held in the loft room of a building at Woodhorn Mill. There were no street lights and many pedestrians carried lanterns at night.'* In one of the stone cottages adjoining the castle there lived an old man called Jobson, reputed to be a miser, but nevertheless a 'man of shrewd and wise counsel' who wore a black and white plaid which streamed behind him in the wind as he walked. The old 'castle' was pulled down in 1908 to enable the road to be widened and 16 houses to be built.

The muddy street in front of the East School in 1917. The school opened in 1913 and the first headmaster was John William Denton. John taught at the North School before coming to the East and is remembered as being an excellent teacher who also enjoyed a good game of football. Under his guidance there emerged some of the most talented young footballers the town has seen. Jackie Milburn was one of his pupils as was Jimmy Richardson who scored Newcastle United's only goal against Arsenal in the Cup Final at Wembley. Whilst the boys achieved great success on the football field the girls scored in the field of music, winning many competitions at the Wansbeck Music Festival.

By 1916 the street from the Grand Corner to Station Bridge had become the main shopping area. Russell Cook, Woolworths, Miss Schollar, G Arrowsmith, W Docherty and R Blacklock were some of the dealers on the south side. On the north side the Meadow Dairy, Amos and Proud, J MacDonald, W Burgess and A Marchetti were in business. Behind these shops was a piece of land called Gallows Hill. In 1294 Robert Bertram, Baron of Bothal, established the right to take felons and hang them within his manor. The execution ground adjoined the boundary separating Bothal and Woodhorn parishes, and was known as Gallows House Close and later as Gallows Hill. An old map gives its location as about midway between Portland Park and the colliery refuse tips along Piggs Moor Road.

The houses and shops in Laburnum Terrace in 1916. A chemist, butcher, tobacconist, draper and insurance agent had shops there, and the health of the locals was looked after by Dugald Revie who had a surgery next to Nathan Rubinstein, a house furnisher. Mining was regarded as an important job during the war and miners were not called up although many volunteered. Women started to do work they had never been trained for and jobs in business were taken over by girls who discovered that they could do the work as well as the men had done. J Allan was manager of the Singer Sewing Machine Company at 2 Laburnum Terrace and he had a busy time supplying customers with material. Clothing was urgently needed by the troops and the Queen had appealed to needleworkers all over the country to send underclothing, gloves and mittens.

The Pavilion, one of the theatres belonging to Wallaw Pictures Limited. The original Pavilion was built in 1910, but in 1920 it was pulled down to make way for a more up-to-date theatre. Plans for the building were drawn up by Steinlet and Maxwell of Newcastle who had already designed some of the largest halls in the country including the Majestic at Leeds. During the summer months the owners put on plays performed by their own company 'The Pavilion Popular Players' and in winter variety acts and revues were the order of the day. The management were described as *'a company who have always endeavoured to place before their patrons a first class show in the most pleasing manner'*.

Children waiting to enter the North School. By 1896 the population at Hirst had risen to around 3,000 and in the following year it was reported that 678 houses would be required for the miners who worked at Linton and Woodhorn collieries. At that time people didn't plan how many children they would have and with large numbers of children waiting to go to school their education became a matter for concern. Elementary education was free and children went to school until they were 12 years old and had passed the 'standards' of reading, writing and arithmetic. The Coal Company built this new school for the children in 1896.

The new houses and cinema at Seaton Hirst. Entertainment was changing and films were replacing the *threepenny gaffs* which were popular in the old days at Ashington. They were plays performed in shacks by companies of actors who put on a different show each night. The Hippodrome was a popular cinema, but this new venture didn't meet with everyone's approval as one critic asked *"whether the fact that 20 prams stood outside a local picture hall at 8.30 pm on March 12th shows that the movies are increasing in favour with the babies"*. The dubious quality of some of the films was also noted as a writer condemned a local cinema whose shows were usually good for allowing *'unclean items to creep in'*.

An old employee of the Ashington Coal Company. Wearing the traditional clothing of the miner, the woollen waistcoat which he wore on top of his shirt and under his jacket helped keep him warm as he went *'in bye'* for there was usually a cold rush of air from the ventilation system. Cloth caps were worn in those days, but officials wore the more protective leather caps. One old resident wrote *'to show how little time we had, my father found me work shortly after my ninth birthday. We had a full 12 hours to work in the mine from five in the morning to five in the evening'*. People were expected to work until they were too frail or ill to go on and an elderly miner did not have much to look forward to, for he was unable to save much for his retirement. Old Age Pensions were introduced in 1909 but until then the elderly had to rely on their sons and daughters for help.

Sinkers at work at Ellington Colliery. In the northern coalfield the circular shaft was the most favoured on account of it being equally strong all round, and when lined out with brickwork or *'tubbing'* it made a first class job. When the size of the shaft had been decided a circle was marked out on the ground a little larger than the finished size of the shaft. If the ground was normal the sinkers removed the soil, clay or rock by digging in the loose ground, and when the rock was reached explosives were used. As the shaft deepened it was firstly completely lined out with timber, carefully levelled all around the sides of the shaft, and brickwork built right up to the surface.

Gilbert Todd sharpening his saw in the joiners shop at the colliery around 1920. Prices had risen sharply in the shops after the war and workers at the colliery wanted a rise. The price of domestic coal had been increased by 14/2d per ton and industrial coal by 4/2d per ton, and this had triggered off price increases on many articles in the shops. Gilbert was luckier than most for he was able to supplement his wages by working in his spare time. Colliery houses were small and many of the occupiers asked him to build wooden back kitchens at the rear of their houses which gave them a bit more space. These back kitchens had a '*stable door*' which allowed the occupier to open half of it at a time and one could often see a housewife leaning on the bottom half of the door talking to someone outside.

Trade was poor in 1930 and the Company was unable to sell the small coal that was produced. They asked their fillers *'to be very careful to avoid unnecessary breakage. Every shovelful of small that is made by breaking up what might be best coal is making for future loss of time and unemployment. We can not go on filling up our heaps indefinitely. We do not mean that small coal should be left in the pit for it is no good to anyone there. We do know that workmen save themselves trouble by smashing coal to a size that is suitable for a shovel, whereas if they would only fill it by hand in big lumps we could get it away and keep the collieries going. If every filler would pay attention to this he would be just as well off himself.'*

A 30 foot cave-in or fall being examined by a company official. One of the dangers in working every day in the mine was that you became so familiar with the conditions that you forgot the possibilities of danger. A new workman heard the coal and strata renting and timber creaking and was very much on the alert, but when this continued day after day and nothing happened he relaxed and ignored it. Less and less care was taken and he would forget to set a prop or fill his tub without taking sensible precautions. In 1930 falls of the roof and sides accounted for between 20 and 30 per cent of all accidents in the Ashington Coal Company's collieries.

Lynemouth Colliery was the last pit to be opened by the Ashington Coal Company. Work started in 1925, but owing to the depressed state of the coal industry in the decade following the Great War it was not opened until 1935. The shafts were sunk during the period 1927 – 34 and only No. 1 shaft was equipped for dealing with minerals. The equipment at that time was the most modern available, for the Company introduced ideas from elsewhere and encouraged their engineers to take a lead in developing better machinery. The colliery operated on an all electrical basis and had pithead baths, canteen and welfare grounds for the workers. With its modern housing estate, churches, inn and cinema it was regarded as a model pit village.

The picking belt where the large stones and rubbish were separated from the coal. After the coal reached the surface it was passed over screens, the small falling through and the large moving on to long, moving belt conveyors. Men stood alongside the belts picking out the stone and coal of poor quality. The large coal was sorted into special best, best, cobbles, trebles and double nuts, lowered gently into railway wagons and weighed. Most of the Company's output was taken to the port of Blyth for shipment. The port was equipped with modern appliances which enabled it to load the coal into the ship's hold with a minimum of breakage.

All the collieries were linked up by the Company's own transmission lines or cables operating at 3,000 volts and the network was supplied with power by this power station at Ashington and one at Woodhorn supplemented by two sub-stations belonging to the Newcastle Electric Supply Company Limited. The length of electrical power cables in use in 1926 was 130 miles, 95 miles being below ground. By 1937 the total amount of cable had increased to 337 miles, 140 miles being used underground. Of the Company's 17 shafts four were fitted with electric winders used exclusively for men, and one was fitted with an automatic electric winder for men and minerals. Six electricity driven fans provided ventilation for the mines.

Some of the lads having a game of darts in the pit canteen. In 1920 the Company appointed a Welfare Officer who was responsible for the Institutes, playing fields and production of the monthly magazine which by 1930 had a circulation of 3,500 copies. He also looked after the canteens at each of the collieries which were opened so that their employees could have their meals in pleasant surroundings. In the 1920's they were mainly used by miners who lived some distance from the pits and by the men on night shift. The canteens sold tea, coffee, cakes, soup and other light refreshments, but there was no obligation to buy.

A photograph taken during the review of the Ashington Coal Company's Corps of the St John Ambulance Brigade in July 1914. It shows them entraining *wounded* at Ellington and W Baker, H Page, J Douglas, G Brown, A Hudson, A Richardson, J Page, E Hunt and R Conway were some of the helpers. The brigade was a civil organisation and was manned by volunteers who wished to help fellow citizens either at home, in the street, or at work in case of sickness or accident, and at a time when they needed skilled help. The order of St John stems from a medieval order, the Knights of St John, and the present order was established in Great Britain by Royal Charter in 1888.

A disagreement between members of the Ashington Amateur Operatic Society resulted in some of them leaving and forming their own society. The Thespian Operatic and Dramatic Society performed at the Miners and Pavilion Theatres, and their shows were well supported by lovers of good music. Their first production was *'Iolanthe'* at the Miners Theatre in 1923 and they appeared regularly in the town until the start of the Second World War. The societies found it impossible to carry on during the war years and the Thespians were not reformed at the end of hostilities. Members of the Ashington societies combined with singers from Lynemouth Operatic Society in 1950 to form the new Ashington Operatic Society. These young members of the cast in one of the Thespians shows certainly seemed to be enjoying themselves.

Jethro Ernest Brown, one of the cast in the Ashington Operatic Society's production of the Gondoliers in April 1923. In 1919 a few people from the town travelled north to see a show performed by the Amble Operatic Society and were so impressed that they decided to start an Operatic Society in Ashington. A notice was put in a local newspaper asking those who were interested to meet in the Presbyterian Church Hall. The Ashington Coal Company, business and professional people showed an interest in the project and the Society was formed. Its main aim was to promote and consolidate the musical talent in Ashington district by the performance of operatic works and to assist a deserving public institution, the Ashington Hospital.

The Reverend Samuel Davidson pushing his bike over the Station Bridge. He was Vicar at the Church of the Holy Sepulchre for 38 years and died one year after his retirement. His obituary said *'if ever it was truthfully said of any man that he loved his fellow men and was loved by them it could be said of him. He had a warm and ready smile for every passer-by whether saint or sinner, was sympathetic and tolerant, but his finest sermons were undoubtedly expressed in the consistent honesty and kindliness of his conduct, for with advancing years deficiencies developed in his speech which clouded his pulpit duties in the closing stages of his ministry. With that affectionate disrespectfulness which is characteristic of the mining community many referred to him as "Old Sammy" which was really a term of endearment because so many were aware of his acts of benevolence.'*

ASHINGTON FOOTBALL CLUB.

ESTABLISHED 1883.

Fixtures and Admission Ticket

FOR 1891-2

PLAYING MEMBERS' TICKET

ADMITTING THE HOLDER TO ALL MATCHES EXCEPT CUP TIES.

JOHN WILSON,
CORRESPONDING SECRETARY.

Thomas Robson, General Printing Works, Blyth.

SEASON, 1891-2.

President.
R. L. BOOTH, ESQ.

Vice-Presidents.

Mr. E. O. SOUTHERN	Mr. H. SINGER
,, W. G. CHARLTON	,, E. GREGORY
,, J. G. WISEMAN	,, J. WILSON
,, W. BLAND	,, T. SOULSBY
,, J. WILKINSON	,, W. CROWN
,, D. ROBERTSON	Dr. BLAIR
,, R. ROBSON	Dr. DUNCANSON

Officers.

First Team Captain : JAMES ATKINSON.
Vice-Captain : WILLIAM URWIN.
Property Custodian : THOMAS CLARK.
Treasurer : THOMAS WALLACE.
Financial Secretary : JOHN FERRELL.
Corresponding Secretary : JOHN WILSON.

Committee.

M. NELSON	J. EASTON	G. BELL
T. CLARK	J. ─────	W. ROBSON

Accidental Fund Officers.

Secretary : JOHN NORRIS.
Treasurer : JOSEPH GREGORY.

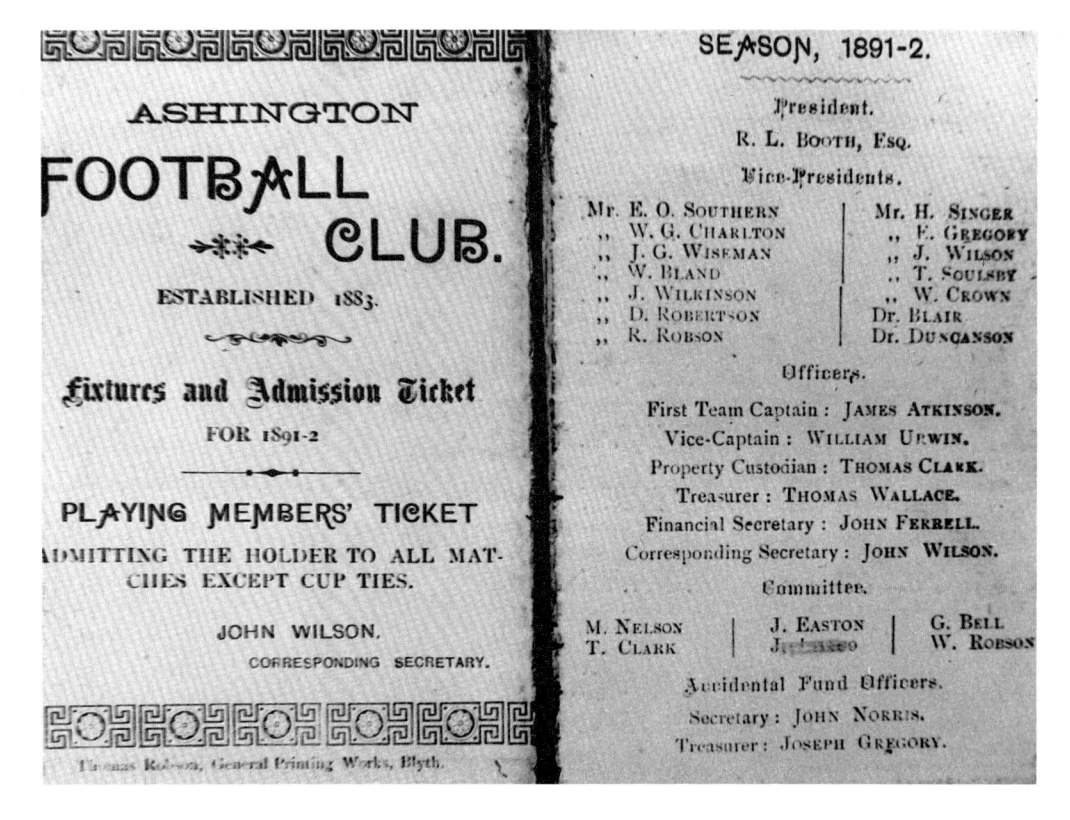

The Coal Company's interest in the town didn't stop with the production and sale of the coal. They took a keen interest in the recreational activities of their workers and their officials, together with approved local businessmen, usually held the most important positions on the committees of local organisations. Ashington Football Club was no exception, the president in season 1891 – 92 being Robert L Booth who was manager at Ashington Colliery for 14 years. The vice-presidents were E O Southern, who later became manager and agent; W G Charlton, who was chief engineer for 33 years; J G Wiseman, chief cashier; W Bland, traffic manager; D Robertson, foreman saddler; E Gregory, overman, and Jimmy Wilson who was timekeeper at the colliery.

The *'Locos'*, one of the 21 teams in the Ashington Collieries Football League. When the Coal Company started the Welfare Scheme they wanted to do something to brighten the lives of their employees and the formation of football teams was one way to do it. They thought that *'there was nothing which did more to help a young man prepare for the game of life than a clean healthy sport played in true sportsmanlike manner'*. Many of the players were under 18 years of age and *'had shown more than an average sporting spirit'* during the football season in turning out at matches sometimes under extreme difficulties. At the end of the season a tea was held at the Welfare when Football League Cups and Medals were presented to the winning teams.

In 1923 it was decided to form a Rugby Club and by November of that year 50 men had said that they would like to join. The Northumberland Rugby Union promised to help the club, expressing satisfaction that the game was to be revived in the town. After three practice matches the club was able to select a promising first 15 and said it was their intention to form a second 15 for they had several good players who were unable to get their places in the first team. Mr J McMenemy, an old rugby player, was appointed coach and the future of the club was assured. Officials and players in the 1924 – 25 season were: F L Booth, J M Henderson, R Whinnom, T Minoughan, P Dunn, A Strong, G Leach, S Adamson, A Prince, A Smith, R Foster, R Booth, J Nelson, H Clark, F Graham, D Barron, F Lees and the Reverend T B Hawkbridge.

Photography was a favourite hobby at the turn of the century and the first camera club had amongst its members F Wiseman (Chairman), R Davis (Secretary), W Gillians, W Hallowell, G Young, F Beattie, J Robertson and Ralph Ward. There were also several professional photographers, the most notable being J T Barnard, Pentland, Dickinson and the Northern Photographic Company who had shops in Station Road and Woodhorn Road. P Curry and Son were also photographers who sometimes got unusual jobs such as taking these men and their dogs. Rabbit coursing had its critics because of its connection with gambling. It was a competition between two dogs, usually greyhounds or whippets, in which the dogs were let loose to chase a rabbit, the dog that caught the rabbit being the winner. Although the sport was condemned there are references to coursing matches being sponsored by public houses in the pit villages of South Northumberland.

Members of the Gymnasts Club practising for one of their displays in 1923. The Company encouraged sport for they believed *'that any particular leader of society, whether director, manager or official, who associated himself with the games and pastimes of the people over whom he had supervision was doing good work, and so far from losing dignity or discipline he was possibly increasing both. The men who had been taught to play the game on the field were learning discipline and control. There was being brought out of him those qualities of coming leadership. The real welfare work was to endeavour to draw together directors, management, officials, men and boys ever working "each for all and all for each". That was what they were striving for at Ashington.'*

Many of the floats built by businessmen were used to advertise their products and the Co-operative Society made full use of the occasion to proclaim the benefits of buying at their stores. This float was built in the yard behind their shop at the west end of the town and Joe Miles, Jimmy McGinn and Bob Black looked pleased with the result. The Society's aim was *'to supply and share with our members the savings and advantages of mutual trading'*. A record was kept of the amount of money spent at the store by each member and a dividend was returned to the customer at the end of six months. The miners spent the best part of their wages at the store and the committee were pleased to tell the public that £25,757 had been returned to members in the preceding half year.

The Ghost Train, one of the floats built by the residents for a Carnival Day parade. The tableaux were a great attraction and there was great rivalry between the different organisations in the town as they tried to produce the best float. Many events were staged to raise money at the Ashington Hospital Carnival. For 6d admission to the Hirst Park one could see a tennis tournament, comic football matches, an exhibition by the Newbiggin Sword Dancers, gymnastic displays by Welfare Teams, folk and country dancing by Bothal Schoolgirls as well as numerous competitions. Many local firms gave prizes for the various competitions and these were appreciated for the hospital was often in a precarious financial position.

It's Carnival Day in the town, and the decorated float is waiting to join the procession to the People's Park. The collectors usually raised a lot of money for the hospital, but in the 1920's things were not so good. The hospital's Management Committee reported in December 1926 that *'financially, as will no doubt be the case with all similar institutions, the hospital has suffered a very severe set-back this year, owing to the industrial crisis through which we have passed and the building programme, which it was hoped would have been by this time commenced, has unfortunately had to be postponed indefinitely. We again tender our sincere thanks to the donors of both cash and gifts in kind, also to those who have so generously assisted with the schemes inaugurated during the year for raising funds.'*

1153 Ashington Colliery Brass Band.

MEMBERS' SUBSCRIPTION TICKETS
AND
DISTRIBUTION OF PRIZES.
TICKETS, SIXPENCE EACH.

John Wilkinson, Printer, Ashington.

No.	Prize.	No.	Prize.	No.	Prize.
1.	Sack of Flour.	14.	Couple of Rabbits.	27.	
2.	Half Barrel of Beer.	15.	Pair of Slippers.	28.	Bottles of Rum.
3.	Meerschaum Pipe.	16.		29.	
4.	Live Goose.	17.		30.	½-doz Knives & Forks
5.	Bottle of Brandy.	18.	Bottles	31.	½-doz. Tea Spoons
6.	Ink Stand.	19.		32.	Couple of Rabbits.
7.	Metronome.	20.	of	33.	Duck.
8.	Paraffin Lamp.	21.		34.	
9.	Couple of Chickens.	22.	Whiskey.	35.	Bottles of Wine.
10.	Beast's Tongue.	23.		36.	Couple of Rabbits.
11.	Couple of Rabbits.	24.		37.	Beast's Tongue.
12.	Duck.	25.		38.	Couple of Rabbits.
13.	½-lb. of Tea.	26.	Bottle of Gin.	39.	1 Hare.

AND VARIOUS OTHER PRIZES.

All Books and Moneys must be returned not later than Dec. 22nd, 1892, to John Dunn, 70, Fifth Row, Ashington, Northumberland. The Winning Numbers will be published in the *Morpeth Herald*, Dec. 31st, 1892. All prizes not claimed within 14 days will be forfeited. Proceeds in aid of Band Fund.

Brass bands have always been popular in mining areas and each band needed to have a healthy bank balance in order to buy the instruments and uniforms for the musicians. In 1892 Ashington Colliery Band organised a Christmas Raffle in order to raise funds, the prizes being donated by local businessmen and some of the more affluent residents. The value of some of the prizes, converted into new pence, makes interesting reading. A bottle of brandy cost 23p, rum 18p, whisky 17p, gin 11p, whilst 1/2lb of tea cost 3½p. The prizes of beer and spirits wouldn't please the directors of the colliery for they were always campaigning against the demon drink.

The Excelsior Band ready to perform in the People's Park. The bandstand was fitted with rolling shutters and was fenced off from the rest of the park which was used for sporting activities. The majority of the residents enjoyed listening to the many bands which played in the park, but they also had their favourites whom they supported on Picnic Day. The colliery bands were paid expenses by the Union on Picnic Day which amounted to a maximum of £3-15s-0d for each band, but because of a shortage of money due to the national stoppage the payment was stopped in 1921 and it was 1939 before a further grant was made. Although the Miners Picnic was not held in 1921 because of the stoppage the band still played on.

The Harmonic Military Band in 1907. The Harmonic Society was formed towards the end of the last century and its two bands, string and military, gave regular concerts which were a huge success. The bands continued to be popular until the start of the Sunday picture entertainments when they had to be discontinued owing to the Society not being able to obtain a hall large enough to hold its supporters. The Society brought some of the best artists in the country to the town to perform at their concerts at the Miners Theatre. Seat prices for the concerts ranged from 2/- in the dress circle to 6d in the back portion of the pit.

Members of the Woodhorn Knuts Jazz Band who also entertained the locals at dances playing more conventional musical instruments. The jazz band was very successful when it played in competitions and usually returned home with a prize. There were 90 bands at the Newcastle Museum of Science for one competition and the Knuts were the only band to win three prizes. The leader of the band was Bob Scott and they used to practice their routines behind Woodhorn pit heap. The band used to put on concerts in order to raise money for local charities and was one of the most popular bands in the area.

Patrol Leader Ross Miles and members of the 1st Ashington Troop of Boy Scouts. The troop was formed in 1909 under the guidance of R Miles, F Maughan and G Bell. Their first clubroom was a loft at the back of High Market, but in 1910 they lost their headquarters through the owners leaving the district. For the next four years the scouts met once a week at Mrs Miles' house in Cross Row. In 1911 they bought their first band instruments, these being two bugles and a drum. The troop had 15 members when war was declared in 1914 and although membership increased for a while many of the young men joined the forces and by the end of the year there were only five scouts left.

In August 1920, 44 boys from the 1st Hirst Troop attended the jamboree at Olympia. Most of the boys were engaged in the mining display, but the troop also furnished a stall of basket makers which was awarded fourth prize in the handicraft section. The troop was formed in August 1908 by Mr J Dorgan and by October 1909 had nine patrols. A club room was built from some old timber from the colliery in Old Lane, Hirst. The troop helped guard the coastline, railway and bridges during the Great War and at the end of hostilities they received a letter from the Chief Scout, Sir Robert Baden Powell congratulating them for the splendid work they had done.

John Scott waiting for passengers at the High Store in 1885. Before there was motorised transport these four wheelers were widely used and had a seat beside the driver and inward facing bench seats for passengers. They usually carried four to six people and there was a larger version called a brake which could seat eight people on each side and was often used for weddings and excursions. John used to take passengers to Ashington and Longhirst stations in order to catch the train. Railway stations were originally built some distance from the main housing development and this form of transport was also used to carry mail to and from the stations, and also collect the daily newspapers which travelled by train.

When the colliery was sunk only a few hundred people lived in Ashington, but with the rapid development of the pits it became one of the largest mining undertakings in the country and more workers were needed. Men came from all parts of the country and the better working conditions at Ashington attracted miners from the local Bedlingtonshire, North Seaton and Pegswood collieries.

In 1880 the Company brought their employees from Pegswood to Ashington by train and although the carriages were open to the elements there were few complaints for it saved the miners a long walk. The *Bothal* was built by J Fowler and Company and was in service at the colliery from 1880 until it was scrapped in 1936.

One of the first lorries to be used by the Coal Company. Their first vehicle was a Model T Ford motor car which was purchased by Mr J J Hall. It was a four seater with a tourer body and in 1918 it was transferred to the Company, the two rear seats removed and a small body added. It was continually breaking down and with poor motor repair facilities at the colliery it became so dilapidated that a new body had to be built. The lorry had brass lamps and a brass radiator and when the sun was shining you could see it coming from a long way off. It was just as well for the lorry was very difficult to control and was often running amuck.

Ashington Collieries Welfare Gymnastic Club about to leave for a trip to Wembley in 1919. The men appear to have been in good spirits as they faced the 600 miles round trip. The Daimler char-a-bancs had a maximum speed of 12 miles per hour so the miners would have to leave home pretty early in order to get to the match on time. At the end of the war there was a boom in the motor bus industry and United organised many excursions and tours. The char-a-bancs had upholstered seats, but they wouldn't provide much comfort for the travellers as they bounced along the dusty roads, for they had solid tyres. Nevertheless there was always a good demand for seats on these trips, especially if it was to see an important football match.

In 1911 the Coal Mines Act made it compulsory for a Mines Rescue Station to be built and in 1912 the committee accepted a tender from Mr Douglass of Hepscott to build a Fire and Rescue Station. It was opened in November 1913 having cost £3,895, the lowest of 11 tenders. The station had a staff of six, an Armstrong Whitworth Rescue Car and a Merryweather 500 gallons per minute fire engine. Instructions regarding the running of the station were issued from the headquarters at Elswick. Fire drills had to be carried out each morning, uniforms, buttons and boots cleaned and uniforms had to be worn at all time when on duty. In its first year in operation Ashington Station turned out to 13 surface fires and two underground calls.

The new motor ambulance being fitted out at the Commercial Carriage Department of the Newcastle Co-operative Society in 1923. The ambulance was able to carry two lying patients, three sitting patients and an attendant in the rear. Splint and bandage lockers and a small medicine chest were fitted inside. The Daimler body was finished in ash and oak, and had mahogany panels. It was described as *'being well mounted and finished in the best possible style, and is one of the best and latest motor ambulances in the North of England'*. The ambulance quickly proved its worth and in 1925 it made 243 runs to the Royal Victoria Infirmary in Newcastle carrying 359 cases. It also made 1,048 runs carrying 1,419 patients to the local hospital.

The steam wagon used by Ashington and Hirst Carriers in Victorian times. It was owned by J Stuart and Son of Choppington who had a heavy haulage business, and there was a great deal of general carting to be done. Much of their work was to and from the nearest railway station for a lot of the material coming into the town was railborne. Bricks, building sand, cement, groceries and household goods were among the loads carried locally. On Carnival Day it was put to another use for it carried a local jazz band in the parade. Most drivers of these vehicles were capable and they needed to be for the roads were in a treacherous state. The slightest mistake and the wagon would get bogged down in the mud or stuck in a pothole.

W Forster's Fancy Goods and Music Shop in Woodhorn Road. The shop sold household goods, toys and a wide range of musical instruments. The shop was displaying a new invention – the gramophone, which was developed from the phonograph. The name phonograph was coined by its inventor Thomas Edison, but the early models gave very poor reproduction and the public in both America and Europe gave it a cool reception regarding it as a valueless toy. The cylinder records were replaced by a flat disk and he fitted a long trumpet shaped horn and patented the invention in 1887 as a gramophone. There was a good demand for the instruments and musical scores which he sold for there were several bands and choirs in the town who gave regular public performances.

In the 1920's a new method of delivering milk to customers came into being. Instead of the housewife taking her jug to the milkman in the back lane and buying a gill or pint it could now be delivered to her doorstep, sealed up in a bottle. In 1924 there were eight wholesale traders and producers of milk and 28 retail purveyors in the town and the Medical Officer of Health kept a watchful eye on the quality of milk sold. Most of the milk was brought in from outside the district and the time lapse in the delivery of milk from the farmer to the housewife caused some concern. Some of it wasn't as fresh as it should have been and the authorities made strenuous efforts to rectify this. By 1927 there were only 16 retail purveyors of milk, but 30 shops served milk over the counter.

A baker's cart belonging to the Ashington Equitable Co-operative Society. The Society had many departments and their grocery, drapery, furnishing, butchers, bakers, dressmaking, tailoring and shoemaking shops provided everything that their customers needed. They *'respectfully asked their members to purchase all their requirements at their own store as increased sales meant decreasing expenses, hence increased profits available for distribution to the customers'*. Although they sold *'the best quality of goods at the very lowest prices'*, their finances were in a very poor state during the 1920's. Members of the store were given credit during the General Strike and the Coal Company was asked if they would deduct the money owed from the miners wages when the strike was over. The mine owners refused and much of the credit was stopped, but the losses sustained during those years were too great and the Society had to cease trading.

Members of the Excelsior Club enjoying a quiet drink in 1926. The club opened for business in 1902 and helped pave the way for the large number of working men's clubs which were to be built in the town. During the first 30 years of its existence as a coal mining town Ashington was without licensed premises for Mr Priestman, an ardent teetotaler, would not allow the erection of such a building. In 1888 a public meeting was called to consider the motion 'Are you in favour of a public house in your midst?' One objector replied 'If you build a public house you build a police station next door'. In those early days the locals had to buy their beer from a hawker's cart which went around the town on pay Friday nights.

A branch of the Co-operative Wholesale Society in Maple Street. Shops were generally smaller then and even the smallest street was likely to have a corner shop which sold practically everything. Window dressing was considered an art and there was a lot of competition between shops as to who could produce the most attractive window display. After the First World War the food that people ate, and the way they bought it, began to change. Food rationing ended in 1920, but it was not until the 30's that breakfast foods such as cornflakes and tinned products became commonly used. Goods packed in the Society's own factories made shopping easier for the housewife for they came wrapped, and this meant that sugar, butter, biscuits and other food need no longer be weighed on the counter scales.

Many types of war orientated postcards were published during the Great War. Patriotic, woven silk and war scenes were common, but this card was rather different. The photographer had taken a photo of Station Road and used his artistic talent to create a war scene. Zeppelins dropping bombs, dead bodies and a ruined street illustrate what might have happened in the event of an attack on Ashington. People weren't as lucky in Choppington in 1915 for a Zeppelin paid them a visit. The exploding bombs broke windows at the Choppington Social Club, Railway Hotel and the Salvation Army Hall in Bedlington. The only reported casualty was a Mr Muldoon who lived in Bedlington. He was struck in the hand by a piece of shrapnel.

Sergeant Jack Dorgan, a training instructor with the Northumberland Fusiliers putting his men through their paces on the training ground. Jack had a lively few weeks in 1915 when the battalion entered the front lines in Belgium. Before going overseas his Company was billeted in the Institute at Cambois and on 29 April 1915 they marched to Blyth and caught a train to Dover. On arriving at Ostend they made their way to the fighting, eventually reaching Ypres. The town was being shelled and Tommy Richell, a postman in Ashington, was hit. The men marched towards the enemy lines through clouds of gas and they later found out that it was the German's first gas attack. The soldiers had no protection against the gas and after being relieved one week later a roll call was held. Only 400 out of a battalion of some 1,200 men were on parade and they had never seen a German soldier.

The Victory Parade wending its way to the Church of the Holy Sepulchre. Although it was a happy time many remembered the tremendous losses and heroism shown by local lads. Hugh Cairns was born in Ashington on 4 December 1896 and emigrated to Canada in 1911. He fought in France with the Canadian forces and was awarded the Distinguished Conduct Medal at Vimy Ridge and the Legion of Honour by the French government. He died of wounds received in the fighting shortly before the armistice and for his part in this action he was awarded the Victoria Cross. His citation said *'For most conspicuous bravery before Valenciennes when a machine gun opened fire on his platoon. Without a moments hesitation he rushed the post, killed the crew of five and captured the gun.'*

At the end of the First World War members of the Northumberland Fusiliers held a farewell dance in France on the eve of their departure for England. The programme included the waltz, barn dance, valeta and lancers. In this country people celebrated in a similar way with Peace Teas being held in every back street. By 1918 queues for food had become commonplace and sugar, tea, butter, meat, milk and bacon were in short supply, but all this was forgotten as everyone raided their pantries in order to provide a nice meal for everyone in the street. Everyone wore their best clothes and the gaily decorated back lane was a complete contrast to the austerity of the previous four years.

Rescue Party (Drowning Fatality) B Coy 9th N.F. Ashington, Ripon, 1909

Members of the 6th Platoon were drilling on the river bank at Ripon when they noticed that Fusilier R Simpson of 'D' Company (Berwick) was in difficulties in the water. Simpson had been playing football with some of his friends and when their ball went into the river he attempted to retrieve it. Sergeant T Smailes tried to swim to him, but got into difficulties and a rescue attempt by Corporal W Kay and Lance Corporal B A Howell also ended in failure. Both were pulled out of the water unconscious, Howell having to receive artificial respiration. Some of the other members of the Platoon jumped into the river and formed a human chain, but the water was too deep and some of the soldiers could not swim. Fusilier Simpson was buried with full military honours at Berwick.

An unusual way to spend the afternoon. Many families lived in flats above the shops in Woodhorn Road and their living conditions were not very good. Large families, the lack of a good water supply and infection caused by the proximity of the ash-pits caused many epidemics. The Workingmen's Clubs were criticised because of the unsatisfactory condition of the conveniences at ten of the 17 clubs in the town. Although the Company's brochure in 1912 had stated that the water which they supplied was good and pure, outbreaks of enteric fever were an annual occurrence which the Medical Officer attributed to the water supply from Ashington Colliery.

Schoolchildren, led by a local band, walking to the People's Park in 1923 for their annual Sports Day. When they arrived at the park each child was given one penny and a bag of sweets. Money was deducted each week from the miners pay in order to provide these small luxuries and the prize money for those lucky enough to win a race. The park was a gift to the town by the Duke of Portland. With an area of almost 21 acres it was used for all sorts of events and had a bandstand, swings and public conveniences for both sexes. The whole of the available space was used for football, cricket and other recreational activity.

Sheepwash Bridge, wrecked by a torrent of water. The winter of 1894 had been hard with heavy snow and a severe frost. A sudden thaw saw the normally placid Wansbeck turned into a raging torrent with the result that the weir above the bridge was breached as the flood water rushed to the sea. The bridge partially collapsed as the height of the river rose 10 feet and flooded the fields along the river banks. The Angler's Arms at Sheepwash was flooded and six months later parts of Bothal Woods were still impassable because of mud and water. The Coal Company had 246 employees living on the south side of the river and they asked for a ferry or temporary bridge to be built so that the miners could get to work.

BOTHAL CASTLE, NORTHUMBERLAND. THE DUKE OF PORTLAND.

The earliest recorded owner of Bothal was Richard Bertram. The estates later passed to his son Robert who, on distinguishing himself in the War of the Roses in which he supported the cause of the House of York, was created Baron of Bothal and First Lord Ogle of Ogle. On the death of Cuthbert, the Seventh and last Lord Ogle who had no male issue, the estates passed to his daughters and eventually to Lady Margaret Cavendish Harley who was married to William, Second Duke of Portland. Their descendant was the owner of the estates when coal mining started in Ashington. It was not until the fourteenth century that the castle was converted from a manor house into a fortress by royal licence.

Bothalhaugh, a rectory in the archdeaconery of Lindisfarne and deanery of Morpeth was under the patronage of the Duke of Portland. Situated above the river to the east of Bothal it was built in 1880 and was a red-bricked building with an octagonal tower on the south-west side. For many years it was the home of the Reverend William Charles Ellis. When Ashington was only a small village the residents travelled to Bothal for their services, but in 1885 the Rector called a meeting of the parishioners where he outlined a scheme for the erection of a church at Ashington which it was proposed should become a new and separate parish. The Reverend Ellis was Rector at Bothal for 62 years from 1861 – 1923.

BIBLIOGRAPHY

Ashington Advertiser

Ashington Amateur Operatic Society 1920 – 1980: The Society 1980

Ashington Collieries Magazines

Ashington Methodist Mission (Central Hall) Golden Jubilee 1924 – 1974: The Mission

Ashington Urban District Council, Official Guide

Beaty G: Ashington: Its Municipal Undertakings, Commerce, Industry and Amenities: A paper prepared for a meeting of the North East District of the Institution of Municipal and County Engineers at Ashington, 27 July 1929

Coombs, W B: A History of the Hirst (typescript), the Author, 1979

Fulthorpe, G: A History of Ashington Mines Rescue Station 1913 – 1981, (typescript) nd.

Hewitson, T L: The Territorial Fusilier Company in Ashington 1903 – 1967: the Author, 1983

Morpeth Herald

Newcastle Weekly Chronicle – 1873

Warn, Christopher Robert: Buses in Northumberland and Durham: Part I 1900 – 1930, Frank Graham 1978